Carpenter of the Sun

Also by Nancy Willard

Carpenter of the Sun

poems by **Nancy Willard**

Liveright **New York**

Acknowledgment is gratefully made to the following magazines in which
these poems appeared: *Esquire*, which published "Buffalo Climbs Out
of Cellar," "Giant Streak Snarls Race," "Saints Lose Back," "Giants
Meet Reviving Eagles on Monday Night"; *Vassar Review*, which published
"Clearing the Air"; *Antioch Review*, which published "A Kind of
Healing"; *Shenandoah*, which published "The Freak Show," "For You,
Who Didn't Know"; *The New York Times*, which published "Why I
Never Answered Your Letter"; *Hudson River Anthology*, which
published "In Praise of ABC," "A Humane Society"; *Kayak*, which
published "In Praise of Unwashed Feet," "How to Stuff a Pepper";
Generation, which published "Dream of Trains"; *Confrontation*, which
published "The Animals Welcome Persephone"; *Poetry Now*, which
published "Walking Poem."

The following poems appeared in anthologies: "Marriage Amulet"
in *Rising Tides* and "The Graffiti Poet" in *The Writing on the Wall*.

The following poems appeared in previous collections: "Guest," "The
Church," "The Insects" appeared in *Skin of Grace*, University of Missouri
Press; "Moss," "Iris" appeared in *A New Herball*, Ferdinand Roten
Galleries, Inc. (Baltimore); "The Freak Show," "The Flea Circus at
Tivoli," "First Lesson" appeared in *In His Country*, Generation (Ann
Arbor); "The Poet Takes a Photograph of His Heart," "The Poet Invites
the Moon for Supper," "The Poet Plants a Forest in His Wife's
Marimba," "The Poet Elects Himself President," "The Poet Turns
His Enemy into a Pair of Wings," "The Baker's Wife Tells His Horoscope
with Pretzels," "The Poet's Wife Watches Him Enter the Eye of
the Snow," "The Poet's Wife Makes Him a Door so He Can Find the
Way Home" appeared in *19 Masks for the Naked Poet* (*Kayak*).

The following poems appeared in the film *Ceremony for a New Planet*:
"When There Were Trees," "A Psalm for Running Water," "Walking
Poem."

1. 9 8 7 6 5 4 3 2 1

Library of Congress Cataloging in Publication Data

Willard, Nancy.
    Carpenter of the sun.

    I. Title.
PS3573.I444C3   811'.5'4   74-13345
ISBN 0-87140-602-0
ISBN 0-87140-098-7 (pbk.)

Designed by Madelaine Caldiero

MANUFACTURED IN THE UNITED STATES OF AMERICA

For Walter and Lillian Lowenfels

Contents

How to Stuff a Pepper

Now, said the cook, I will teach you
how to stuff a pepper with rice.

Take your pepper green, and gently,
for peppers are shy. No matter which side
you approach, it's always the backside.
Perched on green buttocks, the pepper sleeps.
In its silk tights, it dreams
of somersaults and parsley,
of the days when the sexes were one.

Slash open the sleeve
as if you were cutting a paper lantern,
and enter a moon, spilled like a melon,
a fever of pearls,
a conversation of glaciers.
It is a temple built to the worship
of morning light.

I have sat under the great globe
of seeds on the roof of that chamber,
too dazzled to gather the taste I came for.
I have taken the pepper in hand,
smooth and blind, a runt in the rich
evolution of roses and ferns.
You say I have not yet taught you

to stuff a pepper?
Cooking takes time.

Next time we'll consider the rice.

Four sports headlines from *The New York Times*
and the *Poughkeepsie Journal*

I
Giants Meet Reviving
Eagles on Monday Night

Landlord, I've got to move.
You didn't tell me the guys upstairs
are thirty feet tall and could carry
this whole house on their brass knuckles.
You didn't say that next door
lives a sect of bald-headed eagles
who burn themselves every night
and every morning rise from the dead.
I can sleep through the crashing and cawing,
my pictures dropping, my windows snored out.
But the eagles are planning a big revival,
and the giants are giving a party tomorrow night,
and I'm giving notice.
They don't mess with me.
They even asked me to come,
but I'm allergic to feathers,

and I never drink anything stronger than blood.

ll
Buffalo Climbs Out of Cellar

"Will you have some sherry?" asked
the million-dollar baby-faced killer.

He filled my glass, and the whole room
sucked me into its sharkish smile.

"You're fond of hunting," I said.
"Did you shoot all those guys on the wall?"

He nodded and raised the cuff of his pants.
His left leg was ivory to the knee.

"That Bengal tiger was my first success.
Then I matched wits with a white whale

and won. After that I went in for elephants.
And then I heard about the last buffalo

in South Dakota. Very educated.
He speaks fluent Apache. He writes

by scratching his hooves in the dirt.
He's writing a history of the Civil War.

So naturally I took him alive. Day
and night I keep him locked in my cellar.

His breath heats this house all winter.
His heart charges all my rooms with light.

In my worst dreams I see them folding up
like a paper hat, and my dead tiger roaring

and my dead whale swimming off the wall
and my buffalo climbing out of the cellar."

III
Giant Streak Snarls Race

I was running the last lap well
when all of a sudden I see
this guy sneak up behind me.
No, I never saw him before.
No, he wasn't on anyone's team.
He had white hair like fireworks,
he had wheels instead of legs,
six pairs of wings and too many eyes.
Well, I kicked his front wheel
and wrestled him to the ground,
and that's why we had a pileup.
I swear to God he turned into a cloud,
and now I've got this gamey leg.
When my good leg wants to rest,
it wants to walk on the top of the mountain.
The mountain? Who asked for the mountain?
All I asked was to keep in shape.

IV
Saints Lose Back

And there was complacency in heaven
for the space of half an hour,
and God said, Let every saint lose his back.

Let their wings and epaulettes shrivel,
and for immortal flesh give them flesh of man,
and for the wind of heaven a winter on earth.

The saints roared like the devil.
O my God, cried Peter, what have you done?
And God said,

Consider the back,
the curse of backache
the humpback's prayer.

Consider how thin a shell man wears.
The locust and crab are stronger than he.
Consider the back, how a rod breaks it.

Now consider the front, adorned with eyes,
cheeks, lips, breasts, all
the gorgeous weaponry of love.

Then consider the back, good for nothing
but to fetch and carry, crouch and bear
and finally to lie down on the earth.

O, my angels, my exalted ones,
consider the back,
consider how the other half lives.

Clearing the Air

It's been ten years since you tried to kill me.
Biking home one night, I saw only your legs
stepping behind a tree, then you fell on my throat
like a cat. My books crashed the birds out of sleep.
We rolled in the leaves like lovers. My eyes popped
like Christmas lights, veins snapped, your teeth wore

my blood, your fingers left bars on my neck.
I can't remember your name,
and I saw your face only in court.
You sat in a box, docile as old shoes.
And I, who had never felt any man's weight
sometimes felt yours for nights afterwards.

Well, I'm ready to forgive
and I don't want to forget.
Sometimes I tell myself that we met
differently, on a train. You give me
a Batman comic and show me your passport.
I have nothing but my report card,

but I offer my mother's fudge for the grapes
rotting the one paper bag you carry.
In my tale you are younger and loved.
Outside you live in a thousand faces
and so do your judges, napping in parks,
rushing to fires, folded like bats on the truck,

mad and nude in a white Rolls
pinching dollars and leather behinds.
Burned from a tree by your betters, you take
to the streets and hang in the dark like a star,
making me see your side, waking me
with the blows and the weight of it.

Marriage Amulet

You are polishing me like old wood.
At night we curl together like two rings
on a dark hand. After many nights,
the rough edges wear down.

If this is aging, it is warm as fleece.
I will gleam like ancient wood.
I will wax smooth, my crags and cowlicks
well-rubbed to show my grain.

Some sage will keep us in his hand for peace.

The Church

If the walls are whitewashed clean, I hope
that under the show of purity I can find
a mural of monkeys pressing wine,
that below the candles on the choir stall

someone has carved a dancing bear or a boy
riding a wild boar.
The man who makes the dragon under the
saint's feet must know the dragon is

beautiful. And therefore, on the altar,
the Bible will rest on the back of a griffin
to remind you that the beast is present
in every birth.

You shall not exclude them from the communion
of saints and men. If the roof is plain,
put a cock on the steeple; you shall not
exclude them from your marriages.

A Kind of Healing

When I felt you leap, we found you a name.
Though you are all head and belly,
though you have the gills of a fish,
shy and mysterious, you are biding your time.

Though I am a teacher, I can learn plenty from you.
About entrances, for example, and waiting
to show forth at the right time.
"Believe that it grows," I hear myself saying.

"You want to write? You can't name it?
Put it away, let it alone.
Prepare for the coming of ripeness
with songs of Thanksgiving."

O sing unto the Lord a new song.

We are a Christian nation,
we have too many days off for famous men.
Someday, I'll tell you how we marched,
you in me, me in forty thousand,

bearing no flags but the names of the dead.
Living and dead leap in the womb of a terrible war.
Once they too lay nameless and waiting,
now they wait and do not cry when we call them.

I carried the name of a boy from Harlem,
Washington Watson, who left no child
and no great works, nothing except his name,
which I called out to the spiked fence

along the avenues of justice and remorse,
in the great roll call of the dead,
as you danced shameless and merry,
and far away, men gave up their names

faster than any woman could carry them.

For You, Who Didn't Know

At four A.M. I dreamed myself on that beach
where we'll take you after you're born.
I woke in a wave of blood.

Lying in the backseat of a nervous Chevy
I counted the traffic lights, lonely as planets.
Starlings stirred in the robes of Justice

over the Town Hall. Miscarriage of justice,
they sang, while you, my small client
went curling away like smoke under my ribs.

Kick me! I pleaded. Give me a sign
that you're still there!
Train tracks shook our flesh from our bones.

Behind the hospital rose a tree of heaven.
You can learn something from everything
a rabbi told his Hasidim who did not believe it.

I didn't believe it, either, O rabbi,
what did you learn on the train to Belsen?
That because of one second one can miss everything.

There are rooms on this earth for emergencies.
A sleepy attendant steals my clothes and my name,
and leaves me among the sinks on an altar of fear.

"Your name. Your name. Sign these papers,
authorizing us in our wisdom to save the child.
Sign here for circumcision. Your faith, your faith."

O rabbi, what can we learn from the telegraph?
asked the Hasidim, who did not understand.
And he answered, *That every word is counted and charged.*

"This is called a dobtone," smiles the doctor.
He greases my belly, stretched like a drum
and plants a microphone there, like a flag.

A thousand thumping rabbits! Savages clapping for joy!
A heart dancing its name, I'm-here, I'm-here!
The cries of fishes, of stars, the tunings of hair!

O rabbi what can we learn from a telephone?
My shiksa daughter, your faith, your faith
that what we say here is heard there.

Bone Poem

The doctors, white as candles, say,
You will lose your child.
We will find out why.
We will take a photograph of your bones.

It is the seventh month of your life.
It is the month of new lambs and foals in a field.

In the X-ray room, we crouch on an iron table.
Somebody out of sight takes our picture.

In the picture, my spine rises like cinder blocks,
my bones, scratched as an old record,
my ribs shine like the keys on a flute,
have turned to asbestos, sockets and wings.

You are flying out of the picture,
dressed in the skin of a bird,

You have folded your bones like an infant umbrella,
leaving your bone-house like a shaman.

Here we are both skeletons, pure as soap.
Listen, my little shaman, to my heart.
It is a hunter, it beats a drum all day.
    Inside run rivers of blood, outside run rivers of water.
    Inside grow ships of bone, outside grow ships of steel.

The doctor puts on his headdress.
He wears a mirror to catch your soul
which roosts quietly in my ribs.
Thank God I can tell dreaming from dying.

I feel you stretching your wings.
You are flying home.
You are flying home.

Why I Never
Answered Your Letter

It's true I make books, but not often.
Mostly I am always feeding someone,
nine cats whose tails flag me down each morning
and who know a soft touch when they feel one,
and who write on my door in invisible milk:
Good for a handout. Good for a night's lodging.

Mostly I'm taking from Peter and not paying Paul.
My man comes home, dreaming of sirloin.
I ravage the house: three eggs and half a potato.
I embalm them in amorous spices with beautiful names.
It's true I make books, but mostly I make do.
The chapters of hunger are filled but nothing is finished.

At night a baby calls me for comfort and milk.
Someday I'll teach him to sing, to dance, and to draw,
to learn his letters, to speak like an honest man.
Right now I teach him to eat, and I tell him a story,
how an angel came to Saint John with a book in its hands,
saying, *Take and eat. It shall make thy belly bitter,*
but thou shalt know all people, all prophets, and all lands.

In Praise of ABC

In the beginning were the letters,
wooden, awkward, and everywhere.
Before the Word was the slow scrabble of fire and water.

God bless my son and his wooden letters
who has gone to bed with A in his right hand and Z in his left,
who has walked all day with C in his shoe and said nothing,
who has eaten of his napkin the word Birthday,
and who has filled my house with the broken speech of wizards.

To him the grass makes its gentle sign.
For him the worm letters her gospel truth.
To him the pretzel says, I am the occult
descendant of the first blessed bread
and the lost cuneiform of a grain of wheat.

Kneading bread, I found in my kitchen half an O.
Now I wait for someone to come from far off
holding the other half, saying,
What is broken shall be made whole.
Match half for half; now do you know me again?

Thanks be to God for my house seeded with dark sayings
and my rooms rumpled and badly lit
but richly lettered with the secret raisins of truth.

Night Rising

I gave my small son
   a plastic rose
and then forgot.

But in the night
   suddenly he stood
among us. Not

for the bathroom,
   not for water or light,
but for the rose,

which in the night
   he needed. And I
wanted to ask

where he was going
   that a rose, held
like a wand or a mask

could take him,
   and if other faces
waited in that

room, in the last
   traces of clocks
and mirrors

creaking to sleep,
   crouched like birds
which only the blind

eye of the rose could keep.

Walking Poem

How beautifully the child I carry on my back
teaches me to become a horse.
How quickly I learn to stay
between shafts, blinders, and whips,
bearing the plough

and the wagon loaded with hay,
or to break out of trot and run
till we're flying through cold streams.
He who kicks my commands
knows I am ten times his size

and that I am servant to small hands.
It is in mowed fields I move best,
watching the barn grow toward me,
the child quiet, his sleep piled like hay
on my back as we slip over the dark hill

and I carry the sun away.

A Psalm for Dust

I shall never learn to keep house,
to make my bed and then lie in it,
to dust worthy and expensive things.

The dust is myself, how shall I sweep it away?
I learned to write my name on a dusty sill,
and I know the tastiest dishes are flavored with mold.

Today my son brought me a butterfly,
his shirt smeared with the brilliant work of its wings.
I scrubbed and scrubbed, but what soap

can take away the stain of ourselves on earth?
So lovers declare their dust shall be mingled.
So the priest blesses us, ashes to ashes

and dust to dust, we come from the dust of the ground.
In a hundred years you can sift me in your hand,
and from my dust shall rise mushrooms, Destroying Angels,

and someday, a new man.

Carpenter of the Sun

My child goes forth to fix the sun,
a hammer in his hand and a pocketful of nails.
Nobody else has noticed the crack.

Twilight breaks on the kitchen floor.
His hands clip and hammer the air.
He pulls something out,

something small, like a bad tooth,
and he puts something back,
and the kitchen is full of peace.

All this is done very quietly,
without payment or promises.

A Humane Society

If they don't take animals
I cannot possibly stay at the Statler
no matter how broad the beds
nor how excellent the view.
Not even if the faucets run hot and cold pearls,
not even if the sheets are cloth of gold,

because I never go anywhere without my racoon,
my blue racoon in his nifty mask,
the shadow cast by mind over sight.
I never go abroad without consulting his paw
or reading the weather in the whites of his eyes.
I would share my last crust with his wise mouth.

And even if the manager promised
provisions could be made for a blue racoon
I cannot possibly stay at the Waldorf,
no matter how many angels feather the fondues,
no matter how many bishops have blessed the soup,
because I never go anywhere without my cat,

my fuchsia cat in her choirboy bow,
in the purity of whose sleep a nun would feel shamed,
in whose dreams the mouse lies down with the elephant.
I never go to bed without setting her at the door
for her sleep robs even the serpent of poison
and no door closes where she takes her rest,

but even if the manager said, very well,
we can accommodate, for a fee, a fuchsia cat,
I cannot possibly stay at the Ritz.
I understand bears are not welcome there.
I understand that everyone walks on two legs,
and I never go anywhere without my bear

who is comelier of gait than any woman,
who wears no shoes and uses no speech
but many a day has laid down his life for me
in this city of purses, assassins, and the poor.
He would give me his coat and walk abroad in his bones,
and he loves a sunny window and a kind face.

I need a simple room papered with voices
and sorrows without circumstance, and an old lady
in the kitchen below who has welcomed
visitors more desperate than ourselves
and who fondly recalls a pregnant woman riding a donkey
and three crazy men whose only map was a star.

In Praise ot Unwashed Feet

Because I can walk over hot coals,
because I can make doctors turn green
and shoe salesmen avert their eyes,
because I have added yet another use
to the hundred and one uses of Old Dutch Cleanser;
because they tell me the secrets of miners and small boys,
because they keep me in good standing and continual grace
in the ashes and dust of the last rites,
because they carry my great bulk without complaint,
because they don't smell;
because it's taken me thirty years
to grow my own shoes, like the quaint signatures of truth,
because they are hard and gentle as lion's pads,
pard's paw, mule's hoof and cock's toes,
because they can't make poems or arguments
but speak in an aching tongue or not at all
and come home at night encrusted with stones,
callouses, grass, all that the head forgets
        and the foot knows.

The Animals
Welcome Persephone

Coming from the white fields
she will at first see nothing.

They know this and they wait,
the hedgehog, the owl, the mole,

at the mouth of the cave
watching the young queen.

She is saying goodbye to her
mother. She thinks it is

forever. The animals know this;
the owl has sat at many a deathbed.

Only man thinks he can live
forever. Now the air

withers with cold. Behind her,
leaves snap and go under.

By the mineral light of a worm's
eye, the bear's coat shines,

the fish under the earth surface
like diamonds. All who have fed

on the sun come forward,
showing how each nerve

beats with it still, how her death
is not the darkness she fears.

They carry their own stars to the dead.

What the Grass Said

All summer the trees are packing to go.
They engrave their maps on their hands.
They have thousands of hands
and no two maps are the same.

The further they travel, the less they move.
Traveling for them is throwing the maps away,
one by one till they stand naked.
You can see the sunlight through their ribs.

They don't forget to put out buds before they go,
but even that is a way of saying goodbye,
got to make a new map out of my blood,
got to find my home on the mountain.

A Psalm for Running Water

Running water, you are remembered and called.
Physician of clover and souls; hock, glove
and slipper of stones.

Stitch thyme and buttercup to my boots.
Make me tread the psalm and sign of water
falling, when I am going the other way,
climbing the mountain for a clear view of home.

After winter's weeding and the fire's gap in the woods,
first ferns, trillium, watercress,
this vivid text, Water, shows your hand.

The trees stand so spare a child may write them.
You, Water, sing them like an old score,
settled, pitched soft and fresh,
and wash our wounds when we fall.

A hundred Baptists, hand in hand,
rise and fall in your body and rise again,
praising the Lord, whose hand, I think, wears you.

For all this and more my German grandmother
thumped out of bed on Easter and tramped
over gorse and thorn and wild thistle
to the water smiling through her husband's field.

She capped some in a cruet;
        the wink of God,
        the quick motion of ourselves in time,
        flashing! flashing!

Taken in time, she knew, you loosen sin
from the newborn, make gout gay,
turn stiff joints young,
with laying on of your ancient hands
and your wet tongue.

Guest

When you bring in the hyacinth,
the room

fills up with fragrance. At night
if you cross

the place where it prints
its shadow,

it prickles your skin: pasture
and white

breathing of stones.
Come in

Moss

A green sky underfoot:
the skin of moss
holds the footprints of
star-footed birds.

With moss-fingers, with
filigree they line
their nests in the
forks of the trees.

All around the apples
are falling, the leaves
snap, the sun moves
away from the earth.

Only the moss stays,
decently covers the
roots of things, itself
rooted in silence:

rocks coming alive
underfoot, rain no
man heard fall. Moss,
stand up for us,

the small birds and
the great sun. You know
our trees and apples,
our parrots and women's eyes.

Keep us in your green
body, laid low
and still blossoming
under the snow.

Iris

The iris shoot unsheathes
itself crumpled and wet
as the folds of a stomach,

then straightens, summoned
into the elegant blades,
sealed, calked, one on

the other, a print of
leaves, brushed on the
air. This is the tongue

of marriage: we grow,
we cleave without asking.
With our skin

we know.

Roots

This squash is my good cousin,
says the vegetable man,
rolling his pushcart through November.

These parsnips are first class.
I recommend with my whole heart.
I know the family.

Believe me, lady, I know
what I'm talking.
And I give you a good price.

I throw in the carrots free.
Carrots like this you got?
So what you want?

I wrap in the best Yiddish newspaper.
A dollar a year. Takes me
ten minutes to read it,

an hour to read the English.
Potatoes you need, maybe?
My wife says I eat too many

potatoes. In Poland, in war,
we ate potatoes, soup,
baked, boiled.

All my family was ploughed under
except me. So what can I say
to someone that he don't like

potatoes? Positively last chance,
because tomorrow it might snow.
In winter I don't come.

Look for me when the snow goes,
and if I don't come back,
think that I moved, maybe.

I'm eighty-two already,
and what is Paradise
without such potatoes?

On the Natural Memory of Cabbages

Of all green creatures, only the cabbage
never remembers you, because
it never forgot.

Long after you've lost
your grandmother's maiden name,
the blue of your love's eyes,

and yesterday's fiery promises cave
through your past like ashes,
the cabbage shuffles its deck

and finds the day it was born.
It wraps one hour on the next
like a wad of bills.

At the end of its life, it presents
its accounts—*I have taken your time
and have lost nothing*—

and submits its head to be picked,
each leaf unfolded, unsealed
back to its first tooth cutting

a bare field.

And if You Grow a Pure White Marigold, You Could Get 10,000 Dollars!

Into my bowl of puffed rice
fell a packet of seeds, sealed in fine print:
To the first person who sends us
seeds that grow pure white marigolds
we will pay ten thousand dollars.
Chewing, I tasted marigolds
white as silver dollars,
a whole meadow of money!

The sun was a white marigold.
The moon hid a white marigold.
The sky hung out promises of
marigolds white as unicorn's teeth,
subject to the following conditions.
If you find a pure white marigold
in your garden, let it go to seed.
Then send one hundred seeds to us.

That very day I sowed my Almost-White
Marigold Seeds and waited for
mammoth blooms up to three inches across,
flowers resembling carnations, peonies,
white horses, stars, mushrooms,
the souls of snowmen,
the last words of the dead.

The first night I dreamed
of black marigolds, dancing in dashikis.
The second night, of nuns.
The third night, of wind in a cage.
Next morning I saw the first shoots.

It is understood that you will not
give or sell these marigold seeds
to anyone else.
No seeds can be returned.

Not one seed?

My friends, whom I've called up
out of the earth,
shall I sell your children to serve
in the gleaming hothouses of W. Atlee Burpee?
Perhaps he will not know the songs you enjoy,
will not converse with you,
will breed you like chickens with no regard
for your fine manners and finicky moods.

Perhaps you will never see
the shrine of our Marigold of All Colors
having the color of none, a small pod
worn in the buttonholes of tempted saints,
wished on by children, by widows,
carried by the feet of rabbits
and the beaks of invisible birds
from the holy meadows of a nameless god.

The Insects

They pass like a warning of snow,
        the dragonfly, mother of millions,
the scarab, the shepherd spider,
        the bee. Our boundaries break
on their jeweled eyes,
        blind as reflectors.
The black beetle
        under the microscope wears the
blue of Chartres. The armored
        mantis, a tank in clover,
folds its wings like a flawless
        inlay of wood, over and over.

"There is something about insects
        that does not belong to the habits
of our globe," said Maeterlinck,
        touching the slick
upholstery of the spider,
        the watchspring and cunning
tongue of the butterfly, blown out
        like a paper bugle. Their humming
warns us of sickness, their silence
        of honey and frost. Asleep
in clapboards and rafters,
        their bodies keep

the cost of our apples and wool,
        A hand smashes their wings,
tearing the veined
        landscape of winter trees.
In the slow oozing of our days
        who can avoid remembering

their silken tents on the air,
    the spiders wearing their eggs
like pearls, born on muscles
    of silk, the pulse of a rose, baiting
the fly that lives for three hours,
    lives only for mating?

Under a burning glass, the creature
    we understand disappears. The dragonfly
is a hawk, the roach
    cocks his enormous legs at your acre,
eyes like turrets piercing
    eons of chitin and shale. Drummers
under the earth, the cicadas
    have waited for seventeen summers
to break their shell,
    shape of your oldest fear
of a first world
    of monsters. We are not here.

When There Were Trees

I can remember when there were trees,
great tribes of spruces who deckled themselves in light,
beeches buckled in pewter, meeting like Quakers,
the golden birch, all cutwork satin,
courtesan of the mountains; the paper birch
trying all summer to take off its clothes
like the swaddlings of the newborn.

The hands of a sassafras blessed me.
I saw maples fanning the fire in their stars,
heard the coins of the aspens rattling like teeth,
saw cherry trees spraying fountains of light,
smelled the wine my heel pressed from ripe apples,
saw a thousand planets bobbing like bells
on the sleeve of the sycamore, chestnut, and lime.

The ancients knew that a tree is worthy of worship.
A few wise men from their tribes broke through the sky,
climbing past worlds to come and the rising moon
on the patient body of the tree of life,
and brought back the souls of the newly slain,
no bigger than apples, and dressed the tree
as one of themselves and danced.

Even the conquerors of this country
lifted their eyes and found the trees
more comely than gold: *Bright green trees,*
the whole land so green it is pleasure to look on it,
and the greatest wonder to see the diversity.
During that time, I walked among trees,
*the most beautiful things I had ever seen.**

* Adapted from the journals of Christopher Columbus, as rendered in
William Carlos Williams' *In the American Grain.*

Watching the shadows of trees, I made peace with mine.
Their forked darkness gave motion to morning light.
Every night the world fell to the shadows,
and every morning came home, the dogwood floating
its petals like moons on a river of air,
the oak kneeling in wood sorrel and fern,
the willow washing its hair in the stream.

And I saw how the logs from the mill floated
downstream, saw otters and turtles that rode them,
and though I heard the saws whine in the woods
I never thought men were stronger than trees.
I never thought those tribes would join their brothers,
the buffalo and the whale, the leopard, the seal, the wolf,
and the men of this country who knew how to sing them.

Nothing I ever saw washed off the sins of the world
so well as the first snow dropping on trees.
We shoveled the pond clear and skated under their branches,
our voices muffled in their huge silence.
The trees were always listening to something else.
They didn't hear the beetle with the hollow tooth
grubbing for riches, gnawing for empires, for gold.

Already the trees are a myth,
half gods, half giants in whom nobody believes.
But I am the oldest woman on earth,
and I can remember when there were trees.

Dream of Trains

When he was seven, he got a black Lionel
train. All that night he was laying tracks
in the cellar, stopping and starting, trying
the patience of Wabash Pacific, Great Northern,
and Texas Chief. Their hum cleared the dark
like a candle. They ran all night, till the legs
of chairs kicked them over like centipedes.

In six months they'd nosed through the walls.
He heard them tapping the wires, pleating
the asbestos and shaking the beams.
They always brought back news of the interior:
sounds of plaster in transit, his mother talking
to herself, the teeth of love.
So he kept the passage open; they came

and went like cats. Growing older, he set them free.
Now he goes to the game room. Pulling a silver nose,
he maddens the pinballs to light his fortune.
Somewhere are temples built to the worship of travel
and under them, trains buried in tracked cells
are combing the earth and playing his life away.

The Graffiti Poet

Who are you?
I grew up in the schoolrooms of the Dakotas,
I sat by the wood stove and longed for spring.
My desk leaned like a clavichord, stripped of its hammers,
and on it I carved my name, forever and ever,
so the seed of that place should never forget me.
Outside, in their beehive tombs, I could hear
the dead spinning extravagant honey.
I remembered their names and wanted only
that the living remember mine.

I am the invisible student, dead end
of a crowded class. I write and nobody answers.
On the Brooklyn Bridge I wrote a poem:
the rain washed it away.
On the walls of the Pentagon I made
my sign: a workman blasted me off like dung.
From the halls of Newark to the shores
of Detroit, I engrave my presence with fire
so the lords of those places may never forget me.

Save me. I can hardly speak. So we pass,
not speaking. In bars where your dreams drink,
I scrawl your name, my name, in a heart
that the morning daily erases.
At Dachau, at Belsen, I blazoned my cell
with voices and saw my poem sucked
into a single cry:
throw me a fistful of stars.
I died writing, as the walls fell.

I am lonely. More than any monument,
I want you to see me writing: *I love
you* (or someone), *I live* (or you live).
Canny with rancor, with love, I teach you to spell
your name, which is always new,
and your epitaph, which is always changing.
Listen, and keep me alive, stranger:
                    I am you.

The Freak Show

I am Giuletta, the bird woman. I married
the rain man and learned to fly.
Together we walked the high wire
over trees, churches, bridges, green fields,
straight into heaven. We saw the white seed
after a child blows it, and were much praised.
Though I had nothing but him, I craved no more.

Even in falling he blazed like a star.
The next night I went on, knowing I could not fall.
A brave girl, the clowns told me. Then I cried.
I knew that people who never fall forget
danger is all and their blood goes dumb.
Listen, the ring-man said to me one night,
You've lost your shape. You've got no grace.
You're old.

Waiting in the dark trucks I am content to watch,
to nibble the sweet fruits that the dwarf brings.
We walk among the orchards and hear
the silence of tensed feet on the blessed wire.
So much walking affects the appetite, Madam,
says the dwarf with a sucking leer.
And so much sorrow gives enormous hunger.

I am round and simple as a Persian plum,
so earth-shaped now no wire could hold me
or support the weight of my fallow grief.
When you hear the dwarf crying the measure
of my marvelous flesh, you will crowd in.
Blinded by footlights, I hear you wallow
and whisper in the pit below my chair.

My God! Arms like tree trunks cries a man's voice.
Must be hard on the heart, a woman blurts.
O friends, it is very hard on the heart.
For your delight I devour loaf after loaf
of stale bread, till the silken tents sink to rest
and wide-eyed children, bogeyed to bed,
remember my cavernous mouth with fear.

Sometimes I pick at my food like a child.
The taste of the wire in the apple hurts.

The Flea Circus at Tivoli

Let a saint cry your praises, O delicate
desert companion, the flea.
So tiny a mover ruffles his faith
and sends him, scratching and singing,
praising the smallest acrobats of God.

The lady with alligator hips and
hummingbirds in her hair tramples invisible trumpets.
The lights in her eyes dim.
Now from an ivory box her tweezers pluck
three golden chariots and a cycle, spoked
like a spider, drumming the swath of green.

"Behold," cries the lady with delphinium voice,
"Olaf and Alfred and Madame Wu, three fleas
of ancient lineage, fed at my own breast
will race to this miniature castle of pearls."
In the twilight of her eyes, the gold
wagons advance, cautious as caterpillars.

But for the drivers, who can describe
them, save that each carriage moves?
That a golden bicycle whirls forever
toward heaven, moved by invisible hands?
"For those who doubt, here is a glass
which reveals the cause of the tiniest motions."

But clearer than any glass, we believe,
we admire their wizard beaks and their tiny legs
pumping the wheels hard, their gardens and
     parliaments,
pleasing as postage stamps, commemorative,
and we go out praising.

First Lesson

*So I studied the egg, and everything
I learned came from that study.*
                    —CONSTANTIN BRANCUSI

Holding this egg,
        detail
of Quaker plainness,
        familiar
as thee and thou,
        I hold the color and shape
of peace,
        whether blown or dyed,
balloon, promising flight
        that a finger crunkles,
or boxed, the lid raised to show
        a jury noncommittal
as the bald heads of
        a dozen uncles.

The shape of peace
        is the certainty
of the simple thing:
        as when a man draws
one line, known
        from the first
and it opens what we forgot.
        Unicorn understood
from the magnificent horn,
        so I know flight
without wings
        when a candle
against the shell shows
        only a milky light.

45

"Learn from the egg
    and the bird's wing,"
observed Brancusi, flapping
    about his room in red
sandals, his garden of
    sculpted birds spinning
on pedestals like patient
    and sleepy bears.
Tortoise of turquoise,
    birds waking in brass
and silver, harp
    that leaps from the bowels
of Orpheus
    says,

I am a harp raised
    to the first joy of my master's mind,
falling into myself like water
    and sleeping child.
Make birds, wings, planets,
    minerals, faces; nothing you gather
will sing so clearly
    how we are alive, nothing praise
the flight of a bird
    so well as this
round possibility,
    silence unshattered, temple soon
to be raised, the
    ancient Word.

The Poet Takes a Photograph of His Heart

The doctor told him,
Something is living in your heart.
The poet borrowed a camera.
He told his heart to smile.
He slipped the plate under his ribs
and caught his heart running out of the picture.
He told his heart to relax.
It beat on the plate with its fist.
It did not want to lose its face!
He told his heart he was taking nothing
but an ikon by which to remember it.
Then the heart stood up like a bandstand
and the wren who lived under the eaves
left her nest and started
the long journey south.

The Poet Invites
the Moon for Supper

Tonight a stranger followed me home.
He wore an overcoat and feathers.
His head was as light as summer.
When I saw how much light he spilled
on the street, I knew he was rich.

He wanted to make me his heir.
I said, no thank you, I have a father.
He wanted to give me the snow to wife.
I said, no thank you, I have a sweetheart.
He wanted to make me immortal.
And I said, no thank you, but when you see
somebody putting me into the mouth
of the earth, don't fret.
I am a song.
Someone is writing me down.
I am disappearing into the ear of a rose.

The Poet Plants a
Forest in His Wife's Marimba

His wife had a sister, and the sister
sent a marimba.
It arrived with its hair in curling papers
and its back arched.
They petted it calm, it stretched like a dock
lying on deep water and bore
their blows for the tunes on its back.
A rosewood marimba!
A forest of roses!
He plays and remembers their names,
ROSA, ROSALINE, ROSEANNA, ROSEMARY,
and out of the wood they come,
rose trees with flowers like eyes,
with feet like pearls.
If you go in the evening to visit the poet,
you will see the roses
bringing him coffee, laying the table
and singing his wife to sleep.

The Poet Elects
Himself President

Looking about him,
seeing no one more qualified
he elected himself head of the land.
On his arms, ships glided to the sea.
On his navel, the capital raised its dome.
His back supported a lawn, croquet, and decisions.
There were slums and mothers-in-law.
And far overhead he heard the rioting of the stars.
He summoned a net from his hair.
"I will rid the sky of these strangers."
Then the foot said to the head,
Step down, brother, you are no better
than I. The poet impeached himself,
ate black bread, smoked a little, and spoke
in proverbs to delight the young.

The Poet Turns His
Enemy into a Pair of Wings

His enemy was a dragon laced with medals.
It picked his pockets, hid his poems,
beat its tail on his head at night,
blew the nose off his wife's face.
For God's sake, peace! cried the poet.
Then the dragon jumped on his back,
warm in his lizardskin coat he stepped outside.
No one, no one else in the snowy city
wore a lizardskin coat!
Its purple hearts jingled like temple bells.
It rested its pointed chin on the poet's head.
Go right, said the dragon.
The poet skipped left.
Go up, said the dragon.
The poet went downtown.
At one o'clock it turned yellow.
At two o'clock it turned green.
Go up, said the dragon, or let me be.
I am Salamander, fireman of the stars,
bound to cross my brow with their ashes.
How shall I go? asked the poet.
Just as you are, said the dragon,
day in night, night in hand,
hand in pocket, pocket in poem,
poem in bone, bone in flesh!
flesh in flight.

The Baker's Wife Tells
His Horoscope with Pretzels

At dawn he visits the baker's wife
in her Tenth Street kitchen.
Already the ovens are hot.
Already a bride and groom stand up
on the plain face of heaven.
Already birthdays write themselves
on the chocolate cheeks of the moon.

The baker's wife, powdered with fine stars,
ties back the future with pretzels,
hundreds of pretzels crossing their arms in prayer.

"In the house of the archer I see you
teaching the sun to heel.
Though the moon cancels the sign of the two fish,
though she locks the sun in the house of the crab,
though she draws off the nations in tides of folly,
for you the lamb will lie down with the lion,
the virgin will put her head in your lap."

The Poet's Wife Watches
Him Enter the Eye of the Snow

She knew he was writing a poem
because everything in the room
was slowly sifting away:
her dustpan the color of buttercups,
her eyeglasses and her sink
and her five masks praising the sun.

That night she saw him ascend.
He floated above their bed,
he gathered the dark strands
of the poem like a tide.

On his nose her glasses polished
themselves to crystals. On his back
the dustpan fanned out
like a saffron cape.
Now he was turning his face toward the sun
and riding her simple sink into heaven.

In the morning she calls to the newsboy:
"How can I, wife of the poet,
know what he saw and did there?
It is enough that I open my eyes

and my glasses perch on my nose
and show me the brittle dreams of parrots.
Enough that my dustpan believes it shoulders
the broken bones of those warriors the stars,
that my sink gurgles for joy,
and my five masks tell me more
than I knew when I made them."

The Poet's Wife
Makes Him a Door so He Can
Find the Way Home

Nobody else makes doors like the poet's wife.

If she made a revolving door,
summer and winter would run like mice in a wheel.
If she made a door for the moon,
the dead would cross over alive.

Each door is a mirror.

So when the poet loses his way,
crossing the desert in search of his heart,
his wife hoists her lintels and straw on her back
and sets out, feeling his grief with her feet.

She calls up a door that shimmers like water.

She unfolds her palm trees and parrots.
And far away, his belly dredging the dunes,
the poet hears his heart spinning
straw into gold for the sun.

The palms bow. The parrots are calling his name.

He remembers the way home.

About the Author

Nancy Willard is a lecturer at Vassar College and lives in Pough-keepsie, New York, with her husband and four-year-old son. Earlier poetry collections include *Skin of Grace* (winner of the Devins Memorial Award for 1967), *19 Masks for a Naked Poet*, and *A New Herball*. A book of criticism, *Testimony of the Invisible Man*, based on the work of William Carlos Williams, Francis Ponge, Rainer Maria Rilke, and Pablo Neruda, was published by the University of Missouri Press in 1970. Her collection of autobiographical short stories, *Childhood of the Magician*, was published in Liveright's New Writers Series in the fall of 1973. Two children's books, *The Merry History of a Christmas Pie* and *Sailing to Cythera* will be published in the fall of 1974.